ANTHONY E. COOK

THE COOK FOREST

AN ISLAND IN TIME

FALCON™

HELENA, MONTANA

For the memory of my parents, Anthony Wayne Cook Jr. and Dorothy McClintock Cook, and for my wife, Sandy, and my children, Sara and Courtney.

I would like to express my deep appreciation to Robert Bateman and Birgit Freybe Bateman and to Pat Keough and Rosemarie Keough, whose guidance and friendship have helped inspire the creation of this book.

I would like to thank Carl Brenders for his encouragement and for contributing his wonderful sketch of the Cook Forest. I would also like to thank Michael Perlman for his insight, Jeff Wincapaw and the staff of Falcon Press and Mill Pond Press for their generous support.

—*Anthony E. Cook*

© MCMXCVII by Anthony E. Cook
Introduction © MCMXCVII by Robert Bateman

All rights reserved, including the right to reproduce this book or parts thereof in any form, except for inclusion of brief quotations in a review.

Published by Anthony E. Cook in cooperation with Falcon Press® Publishing Co., Inc., Helena, MT.

Library of Congress Catalog Number: 96-93082

Limited Edition hardcover ISBN 1-56044-504-1
Hardcover ISBN 1-56044-503-3

Photography and sketches: Anthony E. Cook
Historical photographs have been contributed from private collections.
Copy-editing: Heather Lang-Runtz

Printed in Japan.

INTRODUCTION

I t has been said that weary voyagers, on their trip from the Old Country to the New World, knew they were within a few days of land when they saw the pink haze of white pine pollen across the western horizon. It has also been said that a red squirrel could scramble to the top of a white pine on the shores of New England and hop from pine bough to pine bough across eastern America to the Mississippi River without touching the ground. Such was the primeval forest when European settlers first arrived. But they soon set about conquering the forest. The mighty trees were felled and burned and the stumps pulled to form primitive fences between the fields. The settlers also discovered that white pine was an excellent wood for working into beams for barns and houses, to saw into boards, and to fashion into the earliest furniture. Three centuries rolled by, and the great forests shrank to small patches until there was hardly a remnant left. As with the passenger pigeon, it was assumed that abundance was forever. We did not notice it was nearly gone until it was almost too late. But, luckily, Anthony Wayne Cook was paying attention in the early 1900s. He had the intelligence and, more importantly, the heart to set aside thousands of acres of this original ancient forest.

We continue to be fortunate that his grandson, Anthony Eaton Cook, is still carrying on the fight for the forest's protection. Nature is not only more complicated than we know, it is more complicated that we *can* know. The more we learn about genetic diversity, the more we realize the importance of genetic variety within a species. It cannot be said that if you have seen one eastern white pine, you have seen them all. The value of the ancient gene pool in the Cook Forest for the pine and eastern hemlock is incalculable for this generation and future generations, not only for the trees but for humans as well. There are many, many sites from which the hemlock has been logged and where this species will never grow again. As luck would have it, however, the Cook Forest is a generous repository of old-growth hemlocks. We will probably never know all of the details of the relationships between the thousands of obscure organisms (such as mycorrhizal fungi) that are in the Cook Forest. It is certainly good to know that they are there, intact, with a heritage stretching back to ancient America.

However, even though this priceless ecosystem is supposedly protected as a Pennsylvania State Park, it is still not free from threats. This land should not be considered as simply a piece of real estate to be used for ordinary recreation, but as a unique symbol of our natural heritage.

I have been fortunate to have explored the Cook Forest with Anthony. Together we have walked the trails that wander among these ancient giants. I have been caught up in his enthusiasm for this very special place and share his feelings of awe and reverence for this precious remnant of primeval wilderness.

Like his father and grandfather before him, Anthony has the intelligence *and* the heart to see to it that this legacy will keep its integrity. He has used his talents as an artist, photographer, and writer to produce this elegant chronicle. His mission is to generously share the gift of this forest and hopefully heighten the consciousness of the general public so that the Cook Forest in its entirety will be protected in perpetuity.

—Robert Bateman

The fronds of the delicate lady ferns contrast with the coarse lichen-covered bark of the hemlock trees.

Scarlet berries from the woodland jack-in-the-pulpit flower and fly agaric mushrooms.

White pine snags and decaying logs help nourish the structural and biological diversity of the old-growth forest.

The knot of a white pine log cradles a red maple leaf in the Forest Cathedral grove.

Wind brushes snow from hemlock branches after an early winter storm near the Longfellow Trail.

THE EARLY YEARS

THE FIRST EUROPEANS to settle in North America surveyed with great trepidation the forests that covered their new world. They perceived the forests as threatening and believed them to possess evil spirits. Clearing the land of these dark primeval woods would provide the pioneers with an agrarian landscape and livelihood similar to those they left behind in Europe. For two centuries the settlers destroyed the forests to create farm fields and erect log homes without regard to the land's inherent value. In the 1800s, the urbanizing of America caused sawmills to devour nearly all remaining forest land in eastern North America.

In the early part of the nineteenth century, the preferred method of transporting heavy and bulky items was by boat, on inland water routes. Pioneers devised new ideas for building canals and using locks to advance upriver. In more remote areas, bulky items such as bushels of grain, barrels of whiskey, and luggage could be moved overland on wagons drawn by oxen.

John Cook first passed through the Cook Forest in 1826 while surveying the Clarion River for the government. He was looking for possible canal routes. The Clarion River had first been explored in 1749 by the French, who named the river Rivière au Fiel, "river of hate," perhaps because it was shallow and difficult to navigate. However, John Cook saw the potential of the river as a water route. He returned to the area later that year and purchased several hundred acres of land.

When John Cook moved into the wilderness to settle along the

Hon. Anthony Cook, circa 1885.

banks of the Clarion River and establish the village of Cooksburg, only about one out of ten Americans lived west of the Appalachian Mountains. There were few roads west of the mountains, and it took many weeks to travel overland from the Mississippi River to the Atlantic seaboard.

Of those hardy settlers who ventured west, including John Cook, historian Henry Adams said: "Stripped for the hardest work, every muscle firm, every ounce of brain ready for use, and not a trace of superfluous flesh on his nervous and supple body, the American stood in the world a new order of man." For John Cook, the greatest dangers from living in the wilderness came with the rigors of clearing the land and developing a fledgling lumbering business.

From the beginning, Cook cut only a limited number of the tall white pine. The trees were cut in the winter and skidded by oxen to Tom's Run, where they were floated by means of a series of bracket dams to the mouth of the stream. In the early days, whole logs were fastened together and floated down the Clarion River to the Allegheny River and on to Pittsburgh. Here, they were milled to supply lumber for the building demands of this growing city.

By the late 1830s, Cook had earned enough capital to purchase his own small sawmill for a few hundred dollars. No longer would he float only logs down the river. A scaffold was constructed near the location of the present-day bridge that spans the Clarion River at Cooksburg to build flatboats. The early boats were constructed to be about 100 feet

Flatboats and log rafts prepare for the journey down the Clarion River from Cooksburg to Pittsburgh. The rafts would float separately until they reached the Allegheny River, where they were often roped together to form a convoy.

Most raft convoys included four rafts and at least one flatboat, which contained the cooking shanty and bunkhouse. This photograph of the inside of a shanty house shows the care and attention that went into building a shanty. Many of the flatboats and custom-built barges were later sold to barge companies in Pittsburgh, which used them to deliver coal down the Ohio and Mississippi rivers.

The lumbering era at Cooksburg reached a peak of activity in the 1880s. With a small pine tree nailed to the peak of the roof of the cooking shanty, perhaps in place of a flag, a raft convoy prepares to embark down the river. The number of workers in the photograph indicates the large number of people who were employed by the lumbering operation. Squared timbers on the river bank await the construction of additional rafts.

long. They were built upside down and caulked before being turned over on the scaffold and put into the river. In later years the boats were built to a length of 170 feet and a width of 26 feet. The boats were loaded with the sawed lumber and docked in readiness for the year's floods, which made navigating the shallow river possible. The floods occurred often enough to allow three trips a year down the river. A small dam built across the Clarion River just below Cooksburg raised the water level in front of the scaffold by 6 feet. This gave the rafters calm water in which to prepare their boats for the journey. When the lumber was disposed of in Pittsburgh, the boats were sold and loaded with coal that was being shipped down the Ohio River.

Of the many children born to John Cook, Anthony and Philip became the most prominent. Largely through the lifelong efforts of Anthony, large tracts of land were set aside and assembled, preserving the forest that later became known as the Cook Forest.

Seven years after Anthony Cook's death, the Commemorative Biographical Record of Central Pennsylvania, published by T. H. Beers and Company in 1898, gave this tribute:

> Hon. ANTHONY COOK, born January 14, 1824, died November 18, 1891.
>
> The Judge was one of seventeen children of John Cook (deceased), who came from east of the Allegheny Mountains. John Cook was twice married, first to Susannah Helpman, who died in 1830, by whom he had ten children, of whom Anthony was one.
>
> Hon. Anthony Cook (known by most people as Andrew) was about four years old when his father took him to where he lived, made his fortune and died. He was reared in the midst of the tall, primeval pines and hemlocks, breathed the pure air of mountains and valleys, and grew to be a giant in strength, six feet five inches in height and weighing 250 to 275 pounds. The principal part of the Judge's education in early life was gained from study at night, after a hard day's labor, by the light of a pitch pine knot. He was a close student all his life; read many good books and periodicals, always read the weekly and daily papers when he could get them, and kept well-posted in politics and the business of the country.
>
> From early boyhood the Judge took a great interest in, and assisted his father in his lumber business. When about twenty years of age, he and his two brothers, Philip and Jerry, began the lumber and boat business for themselves. In 1843 Anthony bought his brothers out, continuing the work alone.
>
> Soon after Judge Cook started in business for himself he began accumulating property by purchasing large tracts of timber lands and also the homestead and the greater part of the land originally purchased by his father. He was careful in management accumulating a large fortune in lands and other property in Forest and Clarion counties, known as the Cooksburg property, on which are erected three sawmills, one flouring-mill, one planing-mill, boat scaffold, several dwelling houses, and a store. In fact it is the best and most valuable timber property, taken as a whole in this State.
>
> In October, 1891, he, in company with Mrs. Cook, and two of his children, Hattie and Wayne, started south, intending to spend the winter in Georgia. They stopped a few days in Pittsburgh and Washington, and when they reached Old Point Comfort (Fortress Monroe) the Judge was tired and they stopped to rest. His great constitution gave way, and on the morning of November 18, 1891, he calmly and peacefully breathed his last.
>
> Notwithstanding the inclemency of the weather, the flood in the river, the number attending the funeral was the largest ever seen in the vicinity.

Anthony Cook saw the commercial value in the timber holdings around his home in Cooksburg—as did many pioneers in the 1800s, who acquired large timber holdings in much the same way. However, unlike most, Anthony Cook did not cut all the forest to feed the hungry sawmills. He had selected for his home an area surrounded by the biggest and best trees. These he did not touch. He loved this forest and chose not to deny it of its crowning attribute. As a result, he reserved nearly 3,000 acres around his home, confining his lumbering operations to the more remote areas of the upper Tom's Run watershed in the northern part of the present-day park.

The same love that Cook had for the woods was perpetuated in many of his descendants. After his father's death in 1891, my grandfather, Anthony Wayne Cook, continued to expand the

This 1893 photograph shows the scaffold used to build flatboats on the bank of the Clarion River at Cooksburg. The boats were built upside down on the scaffold and turned over into the river. If the water was low, brush was often placed on the river bottom to cushion the landing of the boat. The boats carried lumber to Pittsburgh.

Most communities in rural America provided various means of entertainment for their citizens. Here, a band plays on the boardwalk along the river. The Cooksburg Literary Society gave many exhibitions in Cook's Hall, including one program given on September 22, 1871, featuring a musical piece entitled Pocahontas Saving the Life of Captain John Smith. *Admission price for that performance was 25 cents.*

The logs were cut from the hillsides above Tom's Run and skidded to locations along the stream. They were then rolled into the stream bed or into ponds created by bracket dams. Logs were moved downstream over a series of bracket dams across Tom's Run. The bracket dam was an earthen, wood-reinforced structure with a spillway in the center. It was framed by vertical supports, a wooden lined sluiceway on the stream bed, and a heavy beam crossing the length of the dam on top, called the bracket bridge. Wooden poles, called brackets, were placed upright at regular intervals across the spillway. A wall of planks was then placed on the upstream side of the brackets to form the dam. When all was ready downstream, a worker would walk across the bracket bridge and cut the upright brackets to release a flood of water and logs. Often the weight of the water behind the dam would snap some of the uncut brackets prematurely, creating a great hazard for the worker. As the log drive proceeded downstream from dam to dam, it gained in volume and speed. The logs would travel several miles downstream in this fashion until they reached the sawmill, or the logs were carried all the way downstream to the Clarion River, where the rafts were assembled.

At the beginning of a log drive, water is released from a bracket dam located at the headwaters of Tom's Run.

Logs would sometimes become entangled on rocks as they were driven downstream, causing a log jam.

This photograph shows the start of construction of a squared timber raft along the Clarion River near Cooksburg.
The quality of the white pine logs is clearly evident. The men holding the peeves rolled most of the logs by hand.

When heavy rain caused the water level to rise on the rivers north of Pittsburgh, the timber raftsmen would rush to guide their logs to the Pittsburgh market.
The steel mills that made Pittsburgh famous stand along the distant river bank as a stern-wheeled riverboat manuevers around the log rafts.

The Cook sawmill, built to replace an earlier mill destroyed by fire on October 13, 1904. The old-growth forest on the hill behind the mill is the subject of the following excerpt from the Pittsburgh Sunday Post, *December 22, 1912: "And then the antithesis. Within a few yards of the edge of the forest stands a sawmill. It has stood there for 70 years. On the hillside above where the pine is both king and subject we find the leader of them all: 16 feet in circumference; so tall and straight that if cut it would crush the mill below. He seems to have pleaded the cause of his fellow subjects most ably; for while he and they look down on the Cook mill, none of them have gone through its saws. This old monarch and his fellows must have early won the love of the elder Cook and still hold that of his descendents [sic]. Logs were brought for miles to the mill and yet, year after year, this which was right at hand was spared."*

Steam power to operate sawmills in the white pine region of the United States was first introduced in 1832. The circular rip saw was used to saw the logs into boards until the early 1880s, when band saws were introduced to the region. The rip saw was very wasteful, cutting a kerf of more than one-half of an inch; the more efficient band saw cut a kerf of less than one-sixteenth of an inch. As long as timber was cheap and plentiful, the circular rip saw was used. When the white pine forests became nearly depleted in the 1880s, mills adopted the more efficient band saw. The job of each worker, pictured in this early photograph of the inside of a Cook sawmill, required precision. The off bearer, or turn down man, is shown at the right. The sawyer is nearly hidden by the backlighting. The steam-fed cylinder in the middle of the carriage track is in the foreground.

This is the largest bracket dam built on Tom's Run by the Cook family. This dam was located just above the main sawmill and served as a mill pond for that facility. A man is walking across the bracket bridge as two boys practice guiding mill logs with poles.

lumbering business, procuring vast timbering lands in Oregon and Washington. His operations included the 1905 start of the Alaska Pacific Railroad Company, which had the goal of reaching inland to the Copper River Valley of Alaska. These western lumbering operations yielded as much as 1 million board feet a day in saw timber. The vast scale of these logging operations is revealed if one contrasts that figure to a 1949 estimate showing that each year all the trees in the Cook Forest were growing at a rate of just over 2 million board feet per year.

By 1910 my grandfather and his brothers and sisters were facing a dilemma. The family had long ago decided against cutting the forest around their homes, but each stockholder of the A. Cook Sons Company had different financial objectives. To continue holding on to the large tract of forest without income from the property was not practical. Yet the family did not want to sell the property and see others timber the forest lands.

At this time, large numbers of people were visiting the forest on weekend excursions, enjoying the private park preserve as though it were a public domain. If one were to travel from Pittsburgh to the Cook Forest in 1900, most of the trip would have been across the open fields that surrounded the farming communities. Many of those fields have now been reforested with oak, aspen, birch, and maple, but we can imagine what impact the sudden towering wall of coniferous forest would have had on those making the journey from the confines of the city to the Cook Forest for the first time.

Major M. I. McCreight of Dubois, Pennsylvania, claims to have been sitting on a log with Anthony Wayne Cook in late August 1910 during a hike into the forest when the two of them arrived at a solution to the family's dilemma. They thought of preserving the forest as a public park, to "save [it] for humanity's sake." Major McCreight left the woods with tears in his eyes, and a resolve that the great trees should be preserved; he became an early champion of the campaign to save the forest. For many years he spoke, wrote, and agitated for acquisition of the forest by the state. The fight to save the Cook Forest became a cornerstone and symbol of some of the very earliest efforts to preserve a significant part of our wilderness heritage.

Beginning in 1911, McCreight brought the idea of creating a public park before many prominent state officials. In a letter dated April 20, 1911, Governor Tener wrote to McCreight: "It is my firm belief that upon the completion of our state highways, Pennsylvania as a State and its scenic beauty will rival the world. I have no prejudices against lands being set aside as natural parks."

In 1912 a commission led by S. B. Elliot was appointed by the governor to investigate the idea of creating a park and to report its findings to an upcoming session of the Legislature. The commission reported favorably for the idea:

> It is very doubtful if there remains in the United States an equal area of such a stand of white pine. This is no doubt the best. Quite a large area of it is covered with a dense virgin forest, mainly composed of white pine, yet with some first class hemlock and hardwoods intermingled. Besides this area of strictly virgin forest, there are several thousand acres from which prior to 1870 were cut a few of the largest white pine then standing, but where no trees of other valuable species were touched.

Thus began an arduous seventeen-year campaign to save the 7,219 acres of woodland. One of the great newspapers of the time, *The North American,* devoted the entire front page to the subject on February 3, 1913, contributing substantially to the project's popularity. The newspaper wrote: "That for everyone who has seen the forest, it is a masterpiece of nature, which ranks in awe-inspiring features with the falls of Niagara and the Grand Canyon of the Colorado in Arizona."

People throughout the eastern United States began to visit the forest. The project consumed the lives of both Anthony Wayne Cook and his brother Thomas Burnside Cook. There would be many years of struggle before they ultimately secured enough support for the park from the political community.

During this seventeen-year campaign several governors, including Gifford Pinchot, occupied the governor's mansion. In 1911 and again in 1913, the Cook Forest Bill was presented to the Legislature. Both times, the Legislature took no action on the bill. The most common argument against the creation of the park involved economic considerations. Some people promoted the park as a way to develop the local

Above: This 1912 photograph shows several prominent Pittsburgh visitors admiring a giant white pine. This was the first of many trips for the members of the group, as each of them would become involved in the effort to save the Cook Forest. Standing, left to right, C. Z. Gordon and A. W. Cook; sitting, John M. Phillips, Taylor Allderdice, and J. H. Nicholson; in front, Thomas Liggett.

Widely circulated, this booklet was printed to encourage the Pennsylvania Legislature of 1917 to support House Bill 1469, which, if passed, would preserve the Cook Forest as a state park. The bill had the support of the Pennsylvania Forestry Association, the Wild Life League, the Pittsburgh Chamber of Commerce, and many other organizations. It would take another ten years before the bill would see a vote. Finally, in 1927 the Legislature voted for the Cook Forest Bill, which provided for the creation of Cook Forest Park in December 1928.

An early photograph of the Forest Cathedral grove taken from the highway that leads from Cooksburg to the Log Cabin Information Center. Longfellow Trail follows nearly the same path along which A.W. Cook guided guests to see this forest in the early 1900s. The average canopy height for the white pine on the distant ridge is more than 150 feet. This canopy is the tallest found today in the northeastern United States.

Long before Cook Forest became a state park, visitors enjoyed Sunday excursions to the forest. This group, photographed in 1890, is perched on pine logs at the base of a washed-out bracket dam along Tom's Run.

In 1912, the first state-appointed delegation traveled to Cook Forest from Harrisburg to investigate the idea of creating a state park. The group pictured here, led by S. B. Elliot, cruised the timber to establish the commercial value of the forest. The report presented by the commission heralded the idea of establishing a state park.

Anthony Wayne Cook resided in the heart of the forest, where he often entertained many prominent house guests, mostly from Pittsburgh. To introduce them to the forest, Mr. Cook and his chauffeur devised a scheme. As one might imagine in the very early days of motor cars, roads were mostly unimproved earthen paths. The successful navigation of a car along one of these roads was no small task. While giving his guests a tour of the forest, Mr. Cook would arrange to have his chauffeur discover a "problem" with the car. Too bad that something had to go wrong with the car so far from home, but "to walk would do them good," Cook would comment as he led the way into the forest, following a fern-bound short-cut home through the magnificent "Forest Cathedral." The experience would lead many of them years later to join Mr. Cook in the effort to preserve Cook Forest.

economy through tourism. Others encouraged the Cook family to cut the remaining old-growth forest to provide jobs. The Legislature persisted with the idea that the Cook Forest should be preserved only if it resulted in a good fiscal policy for the state and local economies.

A. W. Cook, often working from the Duquesne Club in Pittsburgh, was able to disseminate information on the progress of the project. He furnished a collection of photographs and artists' renditions of the forest for the many prominent conservationists who had recently succeeded in saving a few national scenic treasures during the administration of President Theodore Roosevelt. His efforts interested conservationists Thomas Liggett, John M. Phillips, and Arthur E. Braun. One day in 1912 he took them to his home in Cooksburg so that they could experience the forest, and from that day they worked for the preservation of the woods. In 1915 Mr. Liggett organized the Wild Life League, whose objectives included the acquisition of the Cook Forest as a state park. However, the conservationists were told by most that this objective was unrealistic since federal and state governments had bought mostly cutover lands, never timber.

By 1920 many of the family members had begun to lose faith in the idea of the Cook lands becoming a state park. The ten years of heavy taxation while holding the property for preservation, where it generated no income, had begun to take their toll. On February 20 of that year, a special meeting of the officers and directors of the A. Cook Sons Company was called. It was: "Resolved, that an offer of one of the stockholders to purchase and resell the premises and tracts of land of A. Cook Sons Company . . . for the price or sum of $660,000 be accepted." An agreement with the Goodyear Lumber Company of Buffalo, New York, for the sale of all the timber on the land for the price of $800,000 had previously been negotiated by one of the stockholders—unbeknownst to A. W. Cook.

As a matter of public record in the Court of Common Pleas of Forest County, a Bill of Complaint was filed by A. W. Cook against the other stockholders owning the A. Cook Sons Company. This stopped the sale of the Cook lands. The Bill of Complaint and agreements subsequent reached between A. W. Cook and the other stockholders gave the state more time to act on the Cook Forest Bill.

During the 1920s the debate continued in the state capital concerning the future of the Cook Forest Bill. Alternative plans to preserve the forest were designed and implemented by the conservationists. On January 26, 1927, Anthony Wayne Cook acquired the remaining interests of the other family members in the A. Cook Sons Company. He was willing to continue waiting for a formal agreement to preserve the forest. It would take another two years before the State of Pennsylvania enacted legislation to create the Cook Forest and officially transfer the park property to the state.

In 1926 the Cook Forest Association was organized to save the big pines. It sought contributions from individuals to place the forest in a trust until the Legislature could ultimately appropriate the necessary funds to create Cook Forest Park. Everyone who contributed to the saving of the forest was to be a member.

By early 1927 the Association had collected only a small number of contributions. Consequently, some members were ready to abandon the project. Upon the request of Thomas Liggett, Mr. Cook shaved the $800,000 price for the estate beyond rock bottom by reducing it to $650,000.

Liggett then asked the State Legislature to supply part of this sum. A delegation went to Harrisburg to see Governor Fisher and the legislative committee in charge of such matters. The state agreed to pay $450,000 if the Association would raise the remaining $200,000.

Members were sent out to lead campaigns in various Pennsylvania communities. Industries, clubs, and schools were contacted. The slogan "Save Cook Forest" was heard everywhere.

Donations of money, large and small, were collected across the nation. A. W. and R. B. Mellon gave $10,000 each. The Jones & Laughlin Steel Corporation gave $10,000. Other gifts included pennies collected in the schools. A boy in Spokane, Washington, sent in a dollar. Other dollar contributions came from as far away as Oklahoma, South Dakota, and France. All told, there were three thousand contributors.

In May 1928 the Association had less than $33,000. By December it was within $11,000 of its goal, and A. W. Cook contributed a check for that amount.

An early photograph of campgrounds in the forest, located where the old swimming pool was later built. The State Indian Cabins and the fishing pond occupy the area today. The large building, once the blacksmith shop for the lumber operations, later served the state as a maintenance shop until 1968.

In 1850, the eight states leading the U.S. in lumber production were all located east of the Mississippi River. By 1914, seven of the eight leading states were located wholly or partly west of the Mississippi River. Gradually, the interests of A. W. Cook focused in the western United States. This photograph shows one of his operations in Oregon.

As the scope of his lumbering operations increased after 1900, A. W. Cook became interested in preserving the family timber holdings in Cook Forest so future generations could enjoy the great forests that were rapidly disappearing across the country. In this photograph, A. W. Cook is standing on the road beside a giant redwood in Mendocino County, California. He became an early supporter for the preservation of the magnificent redwood forests.

31

A panoramic view of Cooksburg, photographed in 1912 from the hillside above the entrance to Seneca Trail. The original Cooksburg bridge was built of iron in 1896 and was designed to accommodate the rafts passing around the bend in the Clarion River. The bridge had one of the longest single spans built in the United States before 1900. The buildings photographed in the lower left corner are the Cooksburg store (now demolished), the Anthony Cook homestead, built in 1870, and the boarding house. The boarding house was renamed the Cooksburg Inn and served guests until it was demolished in 1968. The large homes further upstream were built by Anthony Wayne Cook and Thomas Burnside Cook.

Boating on the Clarion River, just above Cooksburg, in August 1896. The familiar outline of the white pine forest on the hills in the background has not changed.

The Association sent its share to the state treasury and, on December 29, 1928, the Commonwealth took title to the Cook Forest. The park became the first acquisition of land by the state for the purpose of preserving a natural landmark. In 1969 the Forest Cathedral area was designated a National Natural Landmark by the National Park Service, U.S. Department of the Interior.

As Major McCreight would recall in his book, *History of Cook Forest,* in 1936:

> Without the staid solid sense of Anthony Wayne Cook, and good judgement backed by dogged perseverance and faith in the lasting good that would come out of it for the public, the Cook Forest never could have been saved; he was so instilled with the principles of his father's teaching with regard to the care of forests, and from the lessons growing out of a century of experience have demonstrated [sic], that he could not and did not yield to the opportunities of his co-owners and business advisers to sell it for manufacture. For nearly 20 years he stood firmly by and watched his and other family members who owned A. Cook Sons Company substance drained away in heavy taxation, interest and constant expense, to save the forest from the ax [sic] that would leave a perpetual scar and desolation of the forest paradise that his father and grandfather had lived and prospered in. It is only fair to say they sacrificed a fortune to save these trees for others.

After the park's official creation, two schools of thought concerning the management of the forest developed. One, represented by the Cook Forest Association, various other organizations, and Anthony Wayne Cook Jr., believed that the Cook Forest should be managed in the same manner as the national parks, with minimal human interference. The other school of thought promoted forest improvement practices such as the removal of lightning-damaged trees and diseased, dying, and dead trees.

For a time, the second school of thought prevailed. The act creating the park had given the state the right to remove "dead and down timber with the written approval of the Governor." Under a plan devised in 1949, the state constructed a sawmill on the park property near the present-day park swimming pool. For several years this operation removed 14 million board feet of dead and dying timber from 600 acres within the park. A great public outcry over this manicuring of the Cook Forest ensued. Ultimately, nearly all agreed that too many healthy trees were being sacrificed by unsound cutting practices. In 1953 the state stopped the operation. Samuel S. Lewis, the Secretary of the Department of Waters at the time, recommended a future policy of "let nature take its course, except when the risks from disease, insects, and fire become dangerous to the forest."

Following the example of the Cook Forest, more land in Pennsylvania was set aside for preservation. In the early 1950s the Commonwealth of Pennsylvania embarked on an ambitious program to expand the state park system. The then Secretary of the Department of Forest and Waters, N. F. Draemel, defined the impetus behind this effort:

> The Pennsylvania State Park system is to set aside for use and enjoyment by our citizens wide expanses of our public lands that cannot be commercialized. A Park system comes under the heading of human conservation, and transcends the commercial by withholding recreational areas from exploitation.

Cook Forest State Park has added acreage over time to include more forest land. In 1951 a vital tract of land known as the "Heffren Tract," located in the center of the park, was donated by Arthur E. Braun of Pittsburgh. This tract is located along Tom's Run and includes the land where the swimming pool is located today. My father, Anthony Wayne Cook Jr., dedicated the property in September 1951 on behalf of Mr. and Mrs. Braun, stating that the Brauns realized that "until this 268-acre tract became part and parcel of the Park, the full and natural development of the Park itself was impossible to achieve." In 1988 the MacBeth family, which has been an integral part of the history in Cooksburg, donated a 30-acre parcel to become part of the Cook Forest in memory of George R. MacBeth.

There will be many more chapters written concerning the history of Cook Forest State Park in the future. The Cook family developed a very special love of the forest surrounding their homes and ultimately a way to extend that relationship to everyone through the preservation of the Cook Forest. ■

Anthony Wayne Cook, in the Cook Forest, resting beside an old friend, a white pine tree.

An Island In Time

THE COOK FOREST

Each time I walk into an ancient forest, I am overwhelmed by what appears to be a dense mass of greenness and a chaotic collection of tree trunks and limbs. The sudden silence—save perhaps for the voice of a blackburnian warbler calling to its mate high in the forest canopy—always leaves me to wonder, nervously: to what extent have I invaded an environment that I cannot possibly understand? Gradually, however, I become attuned to the spirit of the forest and can see beyond its overwhelming greenness to the medley of individual colors and sensations. I yearn to be a part of this natural world.

I begin to see rays of sunlight streaking to the forest floor through the canopy above, allowing the dance of a lady fern to seek the spotlight for a fleeting moment, bright with vivid green. The many colors of a decaying white pine log drying from the morning dew reflect a delicate glow. I hear the sounds of the forest, the call of the warbler, the creak of a tree trunk against a fallen comrade in the wind, the rustle of leaves from an undetectable creature in a nearby rhododendron thicket. A wonderful piney aroma reaches deep into my soul to create an almost alarming awareness of textures and the incredible sensation of being in an ancient forest.

The first colonists along the Atlantic coast saw such an ancient forest stretching before their eyes to the west for a thousand miles. This forest of mixed hardwood and coniferous splendor was generated in the centuries following the northward retreat of the glaciers at the end of the last Ice Age, approximately twelve thousand years ago. Pines grew in a jagged pattern within this vast forest along a beltway stretching between the present-day states of Minnesota and Maine. Along this corridor, dense white pine forests developed in sporadic patches, often only a few square miles in size, after natural catastrophic regional drought and fires opened areas to sunlight.

Delicate leaves spring to life on the branches of a chestnut oak.

White pines reach above the forest canopy on a summer evening.

The monarch of this primeval forest was the eastern white pine, whose straight, resilient trunks served as ship-masts for British ships, which ruled the seas for a time. The relatively lightweight and workable pine timber was also prized by the settlers, and most of the great pine forests fell to the lumberman's axe by the middle of the nineteenth century. Between 1860 and 1870, Pennsylvania led the nation in the production of lumber.

The white pine is the tree around which much of the story concerning the Cook Forest Park revolves. Long recognized as having one of the finest and most significant old-growth eastern white pine forests remaining in North America, the Cook Forest is a magnificent living forest museum.

In terms of size, the Cook Forest is a relatively small northern coniferous forest-type ecosystem, surrounded by much younger mixed deciduous forests and open fields that have substantially less intricate ecosystems. The moist micro-climate created by the dense coniferous forest canopy in the Cook Forest is in part analogous to the great Pacific Northwest rain forests. Cook Forest survives today, a distinctively unique island marooned in time.

Lady ferns and an amanita mushroom.

The Cook Forest is an irregularly shaped area bordered to the south by the Clarion River. The forest extends northward for six miles along the valley and ridges of the Tom's Run watershed. The park itself contains at least 1,500 acres of coniferous old-growth forest, which can be divided into three specific areas: first, the domain traversed by the Seneca, Deer Park, and Mohawk trails above the Clarion River; second, the northern-most corner of the park, consisting of climax hemlock living in a swampy environment; and third, the popular Forest Cathedral along Longfellow Trail. In this area, mammoth white pines rise like great columns from the forest floor, creating an atmosphere reminiscent of the medieval European cathedrals. Overhead, shafts of light pierce the spreading branches and brighten the sombre twilight below, tempering the light of the woods like a perpetual morning. The sunlight rays are captured by the fog and haze in this moist rain-forest-type environment. There is a solemnity that settles upon a visitor as quietly as pine needles falling to the forest floor.

A substantially larger area has been, for the most part, left undisturbed for over a century and is rapidly succeeding toward an old-growth characteristic forest. In the centuries to come, if left alone, this area of the forest will fully demonstrate the old gnarled artistic trees, dead snags (large dead trees still standing), moss-covered logs, and biological

This snag of American chestnut endures more than sixty years after disease ravaged the species.

Hemlock and yellow birch trees flourish in the mossy bog environment next to Tom's Run.

The legacy of a fallen tree is apparent as it decomposes, nurturing young seedlings, fungi, lichens, and mosses.

diversity that are so characteristic of virgin old-growth areas.

Even though the Cook Forest is principally recognized for the white pine forest, a more ancient eastern hemlock forest flourishes on the many hillsides and valleys of the park. Some of these giant hemlock and white pine are several hundred years old and reach upward nearly 200 feet. A sample study measuring the height and diameter of the white pine conducted by forest ecologist Robert Leverett in the mid-1990s found many examples of pine taller than 165 feet, with the tallest reaching just over 171 feet. The forces of nature take their toll on these towering giants. The wind splays and twists the tallest pines, often shattering their upper trunks. This results in the crowns of many trees being toppled as they reach above the canopy.

Ancient forests are some of the richest natural environments in the world. Old-growth or primeval forests differ vastly from younger or second-growth forests in species composition and structure, with the most evident differences resulting from the presence of large living trees, snags, large logs decomposing on the forest floor, and a multi-layered canopy. Old-growth forests are far more diverse, more complex and, to many, more beautiful than younger forests. Life is found under and upon every rock, leaf, and fallen log, as well as in the forest canopy above. Old-growth forest communities or ecosystems such as the Cook Forest are biological structures of diverse plants, animals, fungi, and micro-organisms

Red Squirrel.

that have adapted to their habitats over thousands of years in the absence of large-scale catastrophic disturbance from either natural forces or human intervention. The physical complexity of these biological structures and accompanying genetic diversity are developed as each element contributes to the existence of the whole and the forms of life become mutually interdependent. The plants live in a community in which life is recycled from the many gifts of the sun, rain, and soil.

The large limbs of the pines provide a place for lichens and mosses to grow. Needles, lichens, bark, and other organic materials accumulate and decompose on tree limbs, ultimately decaying into what is known as perch soil, a soil literally perched above the forest floor in trees. Thus, a visitor to the Cook Forest can observe ferns and wildflowers

An early fall evening creates a mood of tranquility among hemlock and beech trees.

Mycena mushrooms grow from a decaying conifer in a tiny section of nature's garden.

growing in these above-ground gardens. Young trees actually grow on the limbs of other trees, a phenomenon seen mostly in old-growth forests.

Old-growth forests are also home to many species of birds. In a chapter contributed to *Eastern Old-Growth Forests* (Island Press, 1996) titled "Functional Roles of Eastern Old-Growth in Promoting Forest Bird Diversity," authors J. C. Haney and C. P. Schaadt present years of study on this subject, including time spent in the Cook Forest. Their research revealed that in old-growth forests brown creepers are twice as abundant, blackburnian warblers are forty-five times more abundant, and black-throated green warblers are three-and-a-half times more abundant. Pennsylvania's rarest nesting species, the yellow-bellied flycatcher, uses mossy bogs in dense groves of old-growth eastern hemlock. Other birds thriving primarily in old-growth stands of coniferous origin include the pine siskin, olive-sided flycatcher, pileated woodpecker, cooper's hawk, and golden-crowned kinglet.

The Haney and Schaadt study shows that old-growth forests provide more consistent supplies of winter forage. Crossbills, northern finches, and other birds that depend on cone crops rely heavily on older coniferous forests. Their work also suggests the importance of perpetuating some of the original habitat preferences of birds as they may have existed prior to European colonial settlement.

Visitors occasionally express concern that vast commercial timber resources are being wasted within the Cook Forest. In commercially managed forests, timber is harvested on a rotation that allows for the specific cutting of trees every few decades. A few even see the forest as a biological desert or waste of potentially vast timber resources, citing in particular the dead and down logs. In reality, the dead and down timber is the lifeblood of this old-growth forest. In 1925 Dr. Willard G. Van Name of the American Museum of Natural History wrote to the Cook Forest Association and A. W. Cook concerning the "dangers and preventive means feasible to maintain [the] Cook Forest in the most natural state." To further quote Dr. Van Name in his letter, "It is on

Eastern Chipmunk.

Rhododendron flowers bloom near Birch Trail in early July.

Erosion and heavy snow cause trees to topple into streams, contributing to the life-death cycle of the forest.

the young seedlings that the future life of the forest depends. Let me assure you that, though the big pines have weathered the storms of many centuries, a few decades will kill them if the undergrowth be cleared away, the brush and dead wood of the natural floor furnishes the nutriment for tree growth."

Few management practices are more important for the long-term survival of the Cook Forest than a policy that will guarantee the dead and down timber will be left undisturbed, even after large-scale windfall devastates the forest's many acres. While the sudden increase of fallen timber caused by wind damage does increase the potential for fire within these relatively small areas, historically that likelihood is remote. The wind-damaged areas should be monitored to determine if increasing insect populations threaten the surviving forest. These populations of insects and invading exotic species, such as the deadly wooly adelgid, harm the natural balance of the forest ecosystem and must be controlled by processes that will have the least negative impact on the ecosystem. The benefit of leaving the dead and down timber for the living forest far outweighs any reason for removing it.

The structure of the predominantly old-growth white pine forest is centered on the dynamic forces of disturbance and succession. The old-growth pine forest within the Cook Forest began growing about 1644, springing to life in areas opened by widespread fires. The young pine trees grew very close together, competing with each other for root space and sunlight. Through this process of competition only the healthiest and strongest trees survive. The dense canopy of the first-generation white pine shields the sunlight from reaching younger and slower-growing trees. The magnificent white pine trees dominate the forest canopy, effectively limiting the regeneration of their own species. Shade-tolerant hemlock trees will grow, however, beneath the white pine over-story. The hemlock are capable of surviving in the dark under-story, growing very slowly, ready to sprout upward, always anxious to fill any gap created by the death of a canopy pine tree. They serve to perpetuate a dominance of their own, due to the ability of the young hemlock seedlings to establish themselves by growing on the dark forest floor. The white pine presence in the forest is nurtured when relatively large openings are created by natural disaster, allowing substantial sunlight to penetrate to the forest floor.

Often, to the surprise of many people hiking in the Cook Forest, the great trees create an atmosphere of spaciousness between them. The trees are seldom crowded and the columnar boles rise for nearly a hundred feet before the first branches develop. The tall giant pines have long ago self-pruned, the lower limbs having died from lack of sunlight and then fallen off. All life appears concentrated at the top of the pines, as the top limbs race upward toward the sky seeking the sun's energy.

Periwinkle and other exotic plants, however beautiful, threaten to alter the natural composition of the forest.

Massive hemlocks thrive on the damp northern slopes of the park.

When an opening occurs after a disturbance in the canopy, patches of dense undergrowth often develop on the forest floor as a result of increased light penetrating through the canopy. A multi-layered canopy is an important structural component of an old-growth forest ecosystem as the younger trees provide a new generation of ready replacement trees when a giant tree dies. Ultimately, when a tree dies after many centuries of enduring the vast rigors of life, it may remain standing for many decades. In the Cook Forest one can still see the twisting trunks of the once-great chestnut trees, killed by an exotic fungus that decimated the species during the first several decades of this century.

The dead snags or standing tree trunks are a vital component of the old-growth forest community. First to inhabit the dead trees are the bark beetles and wood-borers, which carve intricate patterns as they devour the inner bark and wood for protein and carbohydrates.

A leaf-needle-moss composition.

Woodpeckers next help to disintegrate the snags as they excavate larger holes in search of insects. Numerous birds and animals enlarge the woodpecker holes, creating nesting spots and homes. Many other organisms also feed on or inhabit the decaying snags. Ironically, the same snags and logs that seem to some to be merely going to waste actually teem with life. The amount of living material in them may far exceed that in the trunks of living trees.

Many plants and fungi also begin life on the snags. Ferns, mosses, mushrooms, and other fungi sprout to life as they break down and recycle the stored nutrients found in the dead tree. The fungi provide food for many insects and animals, particularly in times of drought. Fallen logs absorb and maintain large amounts of water, helping the forest survive long periods of drought.

The death of an ancient tree drives the cycle of life in the forest. As the needles fall from a dying tree, the gap allows light to penetrate to the lower canopy and forest floor. The sudden increase in energy from the sun encourages formerly shaded hemlock and beech trees to grow with renewed vigor as they compete for dominance in the space opened by the dying tree. On the forest floor the resulting light causes a vitality of new growth and ground cover on which many animals browse.

The moist coniferous forest is somewhat reminiscent of the temperate rainforests of the Pacific Northwest.

Fog forms in the valleys during a late-day rainshower.

Shafts of morning light illuminate the ancient forest.

When a snag finally falls to the forest floor, it may remain in some recognizable form for many decades. As this fallen timber decays, it replenishes the soil, enriching it for future tree growth. The dead logs become nurse logs for the young white pine, hemlock, beech, yellow birch, cherry, and other seedlings. When an area on the forest floor is suddenly exposed to sunlight, often as a result of trees being wind-toppled, ferns grow so densely that they completely blanket the ground, preventing most plants from germinating. The nurse logs that have fallen provide a perch several feet above the forest floor for the young pine to begin growing. The roots of the young trees will gradually reach the ground as the downed logs begin to decay. The young seedlings receive support and nutrients from the nurse logs as the roots grow down into the ground.

A symbiotic partnership that is critical to the self-perpetuation of old-growth forest ecosystems also flourishes amid the decaying wood. The spores of certain fungi, deposited on the forest floor by rodents, sprout to life and wrap their new tissue around the delicate, hairlike ends of tree roots. These fungi assist the roots by serving as conduits for moisture and minerals from the surrounding soil. From the tree, they absorb nourishing sugars and amino acids, which they—being unable to photosynthesize—cannot produce on their own. This partnership between tree roots and fungi is known as a mycorrhizal ("fungus-root") association. A vital part of the organic groundwork, such associations promote the continuation of old-growth ecosystems. The removal of decayed wood from the forest floor inhibits the spread of these fungi.

A birch leaf with white pine needles.

Downed logs also help to stabilize the soil on steep hillsides and along stream banks. They absorb water and provide nooks and crannies in which decaying matter can accumulate and new plants take root. The presence of the logs reduces water run-off caused from heavy rains and snowmelt, which, when unchecked, can lead to massive erosion and leeching of the soil.

The fallen logs lie scattered over the forest floor, no sooner felled by wind and time than they are overwhelmed by other forces of nature. Life in the Cook Forest is a process of recycling as the forest replenishes and nurtures itself from within. All the generations of trees in their turn nourish plants, animals, and other life forms: from witch hazel,

Frost-lined chestnut oak leaves within the canopy.

Heavy snow conceals the rocks in Tom's Run.

Soft mosses and fragrant ferns carpet the hemlock forest.

mountain laurel, and rhododendron to ferns and mosses and fungi; from deer to chipmunks and black bears to birds and insects.

This is how an isolated ecosystem such as the Cook Forest becomes self-sustaining and self-perpetuating, subject to many natural forces that create physical changes over the course of thousands of years. For this reason, every acre of the Cook Forest should be preserved, so that this isolated ecosystem retains enough expansiveness to receive and react to natural catastrophic intrusions that encourage all indigenous species to survive.

Cook Forest State Park has evolved into a forest community capable of regeneration and survival for an indefinite period of time. The distinctly natural process of forest succession that created the Cook Forest cannot be duplicated in the future. Second-growth forests will always have the fingerprint of man upon them. The many natural processes at work within the Cook Forest will continue to flourish in their richly complex environment only if they are allowed to perpetuate themselves with minimal interference from outside influences.

Eastern newts thrive in the moist habitat.

One way in which the Cook Forest and other remaining old-growth forests can be protected is to celebrate them, in pictures, words, and other means. While this book includes such celebration, *An Island In Time* is also meant as an invitation for this and future generations to experience and relate to the forest on its own terms. Celebration and experience of the Cook Forest are, moreover, connected to stricter scientific research projects and can encourage them. Scientists have begun to explore and describe the dynamics behind the development of the Cook Forest's coniferous stands and to document the diversity of plant and birdlife there. Celebration, experience, and scientific research in the Cook Forest can form a symbiotic partnership, helping to perpetuate each other, much like those processes and relationships that make up the forest itself. In this way, the so-far-successful effort to preserve the Cook Forest allows it to function both as living laboratory and living treasure. My hope is that the historical photographs collected by my family and my own color images will contribute to a greater appreciation and understanding of the Cook Forest in particular, as well as a more general appreciation and protection of all old-growth forests. ∎

Two generations of hemlocks and hikers on Mohawk Trail.

A white-tailed deer browses on hay-scented ferns in an opening created by hurricane-force winds.

As autumn approaches, hay-scented ferns turn golden.

The Indian pipe, a wildflower, receives its nourishment from forest fungi.

The fog-laden Clarion River valley on a crisp autumn morning.

In autumn, the light blends the textures and colors of land and water along Tom's Run.

Canoeing on the Clarion River.

72

The great blue heron remains motionless in watchful repose.

Mosses and fungi blanket a fallen hemlock.

Fog rises from the warm waters of the Clarion River as water vapor condenses in the cool morning air.

Perched at the edge of the forest, a great horned owl conceals captured prey with outstretched wings.

Mist settles into the towering hemlock and pine forest.

The full spectrum of autumn colors is revealed as early morning sunshine sweeps across sugar maples.

Sunrise from the fire-tower lookout reveals wind-sculpted white pine tree tops.

In the fall the sugar maples, relatively uncommon in Cook Forest, contrast brilliantly with the other trees.

The Forest Cathedral.

Snags and dying trees provide pileated woodpeckers with shelter and food.

Each fall colorful mushrooms sprout from the forest floor.

Light conditions change dramatically in the forest as wind causes snow to swirl.

Vibrant and subtle colors paint this scene of fall foliage.

The dimunitive blackburnian warblers forage for insects to feed their young.

89

Early morning sunlight touches a stand of sycamore trees above the Clarion River.

Sunlit beech trees add color to the fall forest.

The giant hemlock tree produces the smallest cone of the coniferous trees found in the Cook Forest.

The ornate fruiting body of a Russula mushroom attracts many small animals, which eat the mushrooms and then disperse the undigested spores throughout the forest.

The ancient forest is a landscape sculpted by an ever-changing cast of natural phenomena.